The Dharma of Fashion

A Buddhist Approach to Our Life with Clothes

Otto von Busch

Text contributions by Josh Korda
Illustrations by Jesse Bercowetz

SCHIFFER
PUBLISHING

4880 Lower Valley Road • Atglen, PA 19310

Copyright © 2020 by Otto von Busch

Library of Congress Control Number: 2019946885
Published by Schiffer Publishing, Ltd.
4880 Lower Valley Road
Atglen, PA 19310
Phone: (610) 593-1777; Fax: (610) 593-2002
E-mail: Info@schifferbooks.com
Web: www.schifferbooks.com

Designed by Ashley Millhouse
Cover design by Ashley Millhouse
Type set in Didot LT Std/Proxima Nova
ISBN: 978-0-7643-5894-4
Printed in China

Parts of the interviews with Josh Korda have previously been published in *Buddha Style: A Discussion about the Buddha's Radical Teachings on Fashion and Forgiveness* (New York: Selfpassage, 2012) and *Suffering in Style: A Discussion about Fashion, Addiction, and Endless Aesthetic Cravings* (New York: Selfpassage, 2016).

For our complete selection of fine books on this and related subjects, please visit our website at www.schifferbooks.com. You may also write for a free catalog.

Schiffer Publishing's titles are available at special discounts for bulk purchases for sales promotions or premiums. Special editions, including personalized covers, corporate imprints, and excerpts, can be created in large quantities for special needs. For more information, contact the publisher.

We are always looking for people to write books on new and related subjects. If you have an idea for a book, please contact us at proposals@schifferbooks.com.

CONTENTS

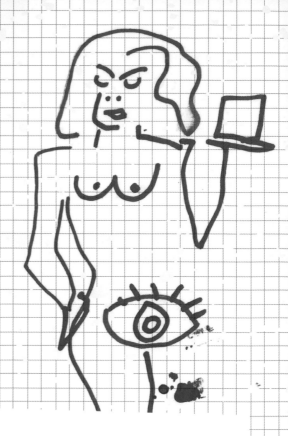

HOW TO USE THIS BOOK:

This book unpacks fashion through ideas and exercises drawn from Buddhist perspectives. Along the journey, you will encounter some of the foundational thoughts of Buddhist practice and have them shine light upon consumer culture, shopping sprees, retail therapy, and the life and death of garments. You will also find some simple exercises that can help guide meditations on your wardrobe and experiences of dressing.

Chapters are typically divided into three sections: an introduction of the theme, a conversation with Josh Korda—a Buddhist teacher—and a couple of meditations.

In the end, perhaps we can think of our engagements with fashion not as an escape from life or denial of death, but as a vehicle towards insight.

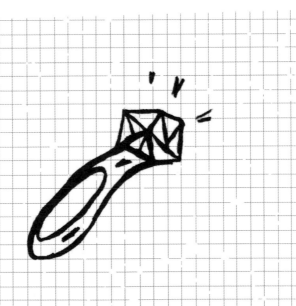

"Where do I find myself?" could be a common question during the search for self—yet we rarely contemplate it. Instead, we skim through the latest collections, seeking something exciting to tell us who we are. We search for a feeling of self amongst ready-to-wear garments, in the feeds of social media, and in the habitual late-night browsing of online fashion outlets. Somehow, we experience the haul from the latest sale, spread out on the bed, to be an indicator of attaining a more secure sense of selfhood.

It may all seem shallow and vain, but could we not use fashion as a better tool for self-understanding?

SNOW BALL ◯

ELEPANT DUNG ◯

01

CHAPTER 1

Aversion

01

The story goes that before becoming enlightened, the Buddha was a young noble in Nepal, free from suffering in his palace, indulging in all kinds of princely pleasures, adorned in gilded dreams. But one day, as he ventured out from the palace gates, he confronted the unavoidable truths of existence: a sick person, an old person, and a corpse. For all his years, the young prince had managed to deny the fate of all life: sickness, aging, and death, and the encounters became messengers to the young prince.

This well-known story reveals how the untrained mind is in a continuous denial of our approaching demise. Our mind keeps itself busy and is always hunting pleasure in order to dismiss that we will all eventually get sick or experience disease, that it is a natural and unavoidable process that we age, and that everybody dies.

Fashion sells us the cure—or at least a Band-Aid. It veils existence in seductive and ephemeral allure, effectively hiding these inescapable facts from our attention.

There is no sickness in fashion, only ideal healthy bodies of radiant complexion. There is no aging or sagging skin, only an ever-recurrent celebration of eternal youth. And there is no death, only the continuous flow of new seasons and collections. The sales are quickly over, and garments that no longer spark joy are doomed to the shallow graves of the dump or sent to the incinerators of sentimental values.

It is no wonder we look to fashion for alleviation. We feel that fashion can give us what we need. We can be beautiful. We can be seen. We can be popular. We can become a better self. And it is so accessible. It is everywhere.

On top of that, fashion sells me an ephemeral sense of freedom, and with each new purchase a fresh wind blows into the wardrobe. Yet my mind is stuck, as if in a continuous loop: "Am I good enough?" "Will I pass?" "How do I get more?" I close myself into an ego-centered loop of aversion and denial, clinging to the passions of consuming youth.

Even if we don't care about clothes, others do; we are doomed to appear before others.[1] By appearing before others, we put ourselves up for aesthetic assessment. Even if we don't judge others by their looks, others will judge us. Even if we never change our clothes, they still speak of some relation to the fashion of our time. It can be both a blessing and a curse. It can offer a sense of aliveness and attention, a thrill of being seen, acknowledged, and attractive. But it may also put us up for painful conditions of anxiety, overload, and addiction.

We crave pleasure and are averse to pain. We are restless. And we all want more. When we leave the fashion boutiques with just the right new things, we beam with pleasure and life. Feeling inches taller than before, we need shades to look into our bright future.

Today, the processes of fashion extend to broader and broader spheres of collective life. Everyone is more or less immersed in fashion, more or less everywhere. As cultural theorist Gilles Lipovetsky posits, fashion sells an image of independence — an ego that *is more fully in charge of itself.*[2] And even more, fashion sells us the *experience* of freedom. Paired with youth, status, and belonging, fashion is, by definition, always the right thing to wear in a certain time. It is always the right thing to do.

It may be a sign of our times that our primary sense of agency and power comes packaged in goods. To most people submerged in the consumer economy, the most powerful sense of affecting one's life is based on what to purchase. Most of us have little influence on the private governance of the workplace, and we are compensated by procuring a sense of agency at the end of the month. Fashion, like freedom, is something we buy.

In the affluent abundance of cheap clothes on trend, we can dress like our idols, gaining temporary access to the aura of celebrities and the palaces where dreams are made. Don't fool

1. Susan Kaiser, *Fashion and Cultural Studies* (London: Bloomsbury, 2012).
2. Gilles Lipovetsky, *The Empire of Fashion: Dressing Modern Democracy* (Princeton, NJ: Princeton University Press, 1994), 190

yourself: everybody desires the pleasures that come with fashion. Even those who do not dare to dream know to love success.

Fashion is often blamed for being shallow and ephemeral. But that is its purpose. The pleasures and allures of fashion lead our attention toward the unencumbered affirmations of life. The iconic fashion designer Yves Saint Laurent is famously attributed to saying "The most beautiful makeup of a woman is passion. But cosmetics are easier to buy." Fashion does not substitute passion; it is an extra layer of affirmation, accessible and transformative as it conveys seduction, aesthetic delights of eternal youth, and lotus-scented oils of hedonism. Such exhilarating feeling of life—at its best, fashion is experienced as the opposite of aging.

Fashion carouses the ego: young, fresh, attractive, and free. But it cannot stop the process of dying.

What keeps you running away?

Most of our wardrobe choices are made with an uncanny emotional backdrop and picked from a reactionary stance. Too often we dress with a sense of anxiety and helplessness. We shop for "safe" looks that are within our reach, already approved by peers or idols. We may feel the risk of exclusion, or possible humiliation may be too big, since we already felt the sharp blades of gossip the last time we made a small fashion faux pas. Not least from our childhood and adolescence, we know the high price of standing out in the wrong way.

Our memories of "wardrobe malfunctions" are carried throughout life. They pollute our mind with judgment, anxiety, and resentment.

Only by seeing these moments, and how today's fears are still anchored in them, can we start to cultivate a more awakened relationship to our dressing habits. Make an inventory of memories and reexamine them with a sense of wisdom and compassion. Annotate a list: Can you trace some of your daily dressing habits to these events?

If we are free to consume and express ourselves, yet still fettered to unhappiness and anxiety, can we really say that we are free? If we do not bring our choices and emotions to mind, are we not simply slaves to the industry, to the opinions of our peers, to our sensations, and to our indulgent habits? As pointed out by Zen priest Shohaku Okumura, we may think we are driving a car, but a more accurate way to look at it would be to see the car driving us.[3] It is the oil economy and the global supply chains that propel the car. It is the politicians, planners, highway construction workers, and advertisers who made our habitual desires translate into continual driving, fueled by our dependencies on oil, wars, and strip malls.

The same could be said about fashion — the decisions of what I can wear are already taken, and my desires are designated, branded, and packaged for me. Yet, I still experience my taste as uniquely mine. With my purchases, I take charge of my life yet remain fully seduced by temptation and desire. But more importantly, my desires are driven by my untrained mind, my stressed and confused thoughts, my habituated delusion of being free.

Many today agree the current model of fashion is not sustainable, and even toxic to the planet. Brands sell more eco-friendly collections, recycle a bit, circulate some materials, and suggest our consumption can be more "conscious." Yet, paradoxically, most of us remain totally unconscious about the psychological driving forces of fashion; the seductive aversion from aging, sickness, and death. It is taken for granted that the aversion, delusion, and greed that reside at the core of fashion are virtues that drive a healthy economy.

Fashion is denial, draped in expensive fabrics.

3. Shohaku Okumura, "To Study the Self," in *The Art of Just Sitting*, ed. John Daido Loori (Boston: Wisdom, 2002).

No society can understand itself without looking at its dark side, and for fashion, this is the realm of denial. The same denial experienced by the young Buddha in his palace. It is a process expressed in obsessive consumerism, compulsively seeking the thrill of the newest looks, the kicks of affirmation that comes with feeling seen and affirmed. The denial at the heart of fashion comes with the admiration of the ego-centered influencer.

We can speculate about what would be wiser ways to be with our dressed appearances, and try to reconcile desire with the suffering that comes with aging, sickness, and death. Can we find more-meaningful ways to be with fashion than a continual cycle of purchasing a very limited sense of freedom? If we unpack our relation to fashion we may understand our lives better. Not only that; our relationship to fashion may help offer some insight to more-general aspects of our everyday lives. Can we transform habits of self-indulgence into insight?

To better understand the possible connection between everyday fashion and Buddhism, I turned to Josh Korda, dharma teacher and recovery therapist at the New York Dharma Punx. We started a discussion on fashion, consumerism, and Buddhism, and what a consumer could do to deal with a destructive cycle of obsessive aesthetic affirmation and compulsive shopping.

INTERVIEW

OTTO VON BUSCH: To put it very shortly, Buddhism addresses the liberation from suffering. Fashion, on the other hand, seems to be a disguise for suffering. What are the timeless types of suffering Buddhism deals with, and what would you say are those that are amplified in our time?

JOSH KORDA: Well, to start, it's important to clarify that there are two types of suffering.

The first type of suffering is inevitable: the difficult experiences in life that one can do nothing about. For example: aging, sickness, death, being separated from those we love, being stuck with difficult people, the daily frustrations of impoliteness, etc.

In addition to the stress that the above produces, there's a second type of unnecessary suffering: self-centered thought, why me? How can I stop this from happening?, escapist ideation, obsessive planning and worrying, addiction to distractions, feeding off our emotional resistance and drama, etc.

This latter type of suffering is what Buddhism alleviates. And yes, the place and time we live in tends to exaggerate suffering. Our culture celebrates youth, beauty, success, and a type of homogenized happiness based on accumulation and greed; we hide the elderly in assisted-living facilities and nursing homes, the sick in hospitals; the dead are whisked away and then dressed up to look like they're sleeping, or cremated out of view. The poor are ghettoized. All of the above sets us up for a lot of suffering when the inevitable setbacks of life occur.

OVB: As I understand it, sometimes suffering is translated as dissatisfaction. I see an obvious connection to fashion, as most often fashion makes us feel continuously incomplete (without the latest must-haves), and it seems fashion is there to fuel this fire of unsatisfied desires. How should we relate to this kind of suffering or dissatisfaction?

JK: Craving for quick, easy, sensual pleasure (or *tanha* in Pali) is a default setting for the mind. In addition to lives crammed with responsibilities, the mind in and of itself torments us with unrealistic fears and expectations; worn down and unhappy, we want happiness to be something that comes from the swipe of a credit card. As a result, our craving is further fueled by the unsatisfactory nature (*dukkha*) of the short-term, conditional pleasures we find in our consumer lifestyles. We're continually frustrated when we seek happiness in what the Buddha called the worldly winds that blow us about: success and fame; accumulation of goods, such as gadgets and fashionable apparel; approval from others; sex, drugs, alcohol, and other short-term relishes. Such endeavors only temporarily divert our attention from the underlying stress that builds up in our stressful lives: the myriad responsibilities, vulnerable careers, the shadows of financial uncertainty. Indeed, the result is we do feel there's something missing, as the relief we seek is so rarely found externally.

Sure, fashion marketing might exacerbate our underlying feeling of something missing (Look! The reason you're not beautiful and universally loved is because you don't own a Louis Vuitton this or a Helmut Lang that). But it's hardly the main culprit; again, it's the nature of our default programming.

The way to relate to unsatisfactoriness of external pleasures is to:

- Look at our priorities. It's essential to reduce the stress that results from workaholism, addictions, unrealistic expectations that relationships will "fix us." We rebalance our lives to include a greater emphasis on endeavors that create lasting peace of mind: friendship, volunteerism, body awareness such as yoga, and, of course, spiritual practice.

- Throughout the day, work on reducing stress by noting how we can calm our breath and body, and how we can refocus our mind on perceptions that don't cause unnecessary tension.

- Work on developing antidotes to our fear-driven, competitive default mind states: we practice forgiveness, kindness, appreciation of other's happiness, compassion.

- Have a strong moral foundation to our lives that we won't cross. The less harm we cause, the less callous our relationship with strangers, the less shame and guilt we carry.

- A daily meditation practice, based on learning to find ease internally, regardless of our agitation and inevitable stressors.

OVB: When it comes to temptation, sometimes when we encounter a garment we like, we feel we just *NEED* it, that we can't live without this newly dressed "me." What would be a skillful way to respond to this?

JK: To become aware of the attraction to the garment as early as possible, before too much "Papañca" (obsessive thought) has developed. It's important to note that attraction first arises physically, as gut feelings, which are—interestingly enough—how the unconscious alerts us to the presence of something desirable or dangerous, then rises to the mind, which focuses on an object then begins to add stories: "I deserve that. After all, I work hard, I never get my fair share," etc. If we can mindfully watch how the body reacts to beauty, note how the sensations arise, linger, then eventually pass, without focusing on all the thought-based chatter, it's actually quite possible, with practice, to resist following urges and impulses.

OVB: So is fasting and refusal of fashion the best way? It is easy to think fashion is all about gluttony and greed, but austerity and minimalism in the form of fasting and asceticism are recurring techniques in fashion too, and also in many religions. But doesn't it also lead to other forms of disconnection and denial? What place does asceticism have in Buddhism?

JK: Balanced asceticism, or more properly put, renunciation, is often misunderstood, seen as a type of self-punishment or denial. It's actually a search for true joy and happiness by putting aside, where possible, what we don't need, especially when we've become addicted or dependent. The Buddha taught we all require certain essentials: enough food, clothing, shelter, and medicine to keep us healthy and alert, so that we can live productive lives and cultivate inner peace. We can even enjoy the benefits of our hard work, so long as we don't get caught up in accumulation, addicted to commodities that aren't essential to peace of mind. People can get so easily bent out of shape when they can't get a cell phone signal or a call gets dropped, when the internet goes out, when our routines become interrupted. When this happens, we know we're imbalanced.

OVB: In a way we might say fashion is honest about its impermanence. Everyone knows fashions are fleeting. Could there be a way for us to use this honest impermanence in meditation? I am thinking about how Buddhists are encouraged to meditate over an image of a corpse, in order to better understand impermanence—could we encourage designers to meditate over last season's sales as a path toward enlightenment? What other Buddhist exercises may help expose our impermanence?

JK: From what I've seen, designers tend to feed on drama, stress, and adrenaline (running out of time, materials not being up to quality, no one's helping me, etc., etc.) as a way to stay focused and energized over the long hours that lead up to a presentation deadline. The longtime result is a mind that brings agitation and stress into every facet of life; drama and stress, of course, demands and feeds on conflict; it takes its toll on relationships, friendships, etc. over the years—an inability to enjoy peace.

I'd first suggest exercises that demonstrate how one can be productive and creative without introducing unnecessary hysterical narratives into the mix: breathing deeply, relaxing areas of the body that carry stress, focusing on present efforts without carrying extraneous "to-do" lists, etc. People find, when they're taught stress reduction techniques, that they can get more work done, and at less of a toll, than when their process involves agitation, moaning, complaining, etc.

Additionally, an occasional meditation asking designers to bring to mind whatever drama or agitation was dominating their lives a year ago, two years ago, etc. Inevitably they'll find that few of the excitations, which seemed so important and essential earlier, are remotely memorable.

What makes something feel "right"?

Our social bonds ensnare our awareness, and we often come to identify with the role others have given us without being aware of how we got there. Our sense of selfhood is seduced by the safety that comes with being "right," and fashion is always right. We become observers of our lives, rarely letting go enough to actually experience the strings that fetter us to the opinions of our peers. You may tell yourself you picked your style, but it may not always be so if you examine your choices critically. Who are the peers whose judgment you seek and listen to? Are they a part in choosing what you feel is "right"?

Fashion is to a large degree fueled by envy and jealousy, yet these emotions are often tainted by shame, and we seldom dare to articulate or engage with these emotions. Make a list of where clothes have made you feel superior and better than others. Make a second list of where clothes have made you feel inferior and less than others.

CHAPTER 2

Craving Style

It is said that on the eve of his enlightenment, the Buddha sat beneath a tree and was assailed by the demon Mara. Mara is literally "Death," the personification of temptation and distraction. Using seductive images and ultimately doubt, Mara challenged the Buddha, distracting him from his goal of enlightenment. After several unsuccessful attempts, Mara retreated. By knowing and seeing Mara with unhindered attention, the Buddha could turn the demon away.

Mara is always within us. The demon represents everyday experiences, such as fear, temptation, anxiety, relationship difficulties, and addiction. These are just some of all the afflictions we meet in the landscape of our minds: restlessness and anxiety, desire and craving, aversion and delusion, and, finally, doubt. Mara urges us to avoid all the unpleasant mind states that accompany the path toward healing and awakening and instead engorge in all temptation for pleasure.

It is not foreign to draw parallels to fashion. Like fashion, Mara is what tempts us, and cannot be overcome with simple denial.

Rather than applying brute force, which is useless against temptation and craving, the Buddha's example suggests approaching Mara with the spirit of listening and transformation. Mara can be won over with weapons of compassion, equanimity, appreciation, and, ultimately, insight, in order to establish sovereignty of our own minds.

Fashion is fueled by our desires, and in many ways, we dress to become our desires. But uncontrolled desire combined with our hunger for attachment easily turns into craving. We spot an attractive friend crossing the road in just that right thing, making him or her stand out as a mirage of perfection. We may not spell it out, but the rush in the body cries "I need that too!" The look appears to us as a ticket to that world, a signature texted at a postcard from a place of allure. A low-level fever runs through my body; "I need to find that outfit!" Passion can be almost indistinguishable from a fever, so no wonder that fashion is such an incubator to that pleasant sickness of consumerism.

Not unlike how Mara bedevils the Buddha, it can be fruitful to think that fashion is not entirely chosen by us, but it assails us, is inflicted upon us.

But does that necessarily mean we are "victims" or "slaves" to fashion?

The idea that consumers are subjects to some forms of submission to aesthetic power may not be inaccurate. However, the framing of the relationship as master/slave may shy away from the complex social relationships that fashion and consumerism flourish in.

"I was absolute master in my old dressing gown," philosopher Denis Diderot famously put it, "but I have become a slave to my new one," since he felt the need to update his whole wardrobe because of one new piece. We may think we choose fashion from our free will, but with just a little bit of self-observation, we find ourselves subjected to the tastes of our peers, our habits, and our confused minds. And as with a new dressing gown, our desires creep upward, ever wanting more.

But today's fashion consumers don't see themselves as slaves. Instead, we are continually sold aesthetic rebellion and independence. We do not submit to fashion; we crave fashion. We celebrate impulse buying and happily engage in retail therapy. Fashion is not about subordination as much as a site for tension, anxiety release, and soothing from stress.

And even as we cannot escape the news of environmental impact of mass consumerism, we keep shopping. Perhaps it is true, as Buddhist ecologist Stephanie Keza argues, that we are stricken by a "sickness of consumerism," a spiritual disease of unquenchable consumption, poisoning, and denial?[4]

4. Stephanie Keza, ed., *Hooked! Buddhist Writings on Greed, Desire, and the Urge to Consume* (Boston: Shambhala, 2005).

But don't we also crave fashion because it is a little forbidden, that it flirts with danger, the gamble of the passions? Fashion is the antipode to frugality, and some shame is still bound to the blatant egotism of fully and flamboyantly celebrating one's desires, which may still be the model of orgiastic pleasure. Indeed, isn't fashion partly about the pleasure of challenging virtue, gluttonous delight, and a thrill in greedy jealousy, to envelope ourselves in virtuous sin, taking sartorial risk and challenging the fates? It is the kick that makes me feel more alive, if only for a short while.

We shop, dress up, feel the hungry eyes of our peers, and the brain's reward system runs on the highest levels. As I leave the store with the new goods, I feel like a conqueror and experience the emotional kick that comes with gaining a few notches in the gamble of attention. As Buddhist scholar Robert Thurman points out, even when wearing masks, the sense of "I" is still in its own world of sensations:

> When "I" feel proud, I soar above others.
> When "I" feel jealous, I am brought down into
> a nagging dislike of another. Guilt, fear, greed,
> confusion, even determination — all these
> energies seem to take hold of "me," or seems to
> emanate from "I." But as I think them through,
> observe them in actuality or in memory, they seem
> fully bound in relationships.[5]

This focus on the "I" leads not only to self-identification and self-indulgence, but to the prejudice that all others are nonself, that they are wrong or worse than the universe of the self-centered "me." Being at the center of the universe makes it seem perfectly normal to be drawn into greed, envy, and jealousy. Yet, these mental processes of comparison feed the judging aspects of our mind. For a self-centered mind, the success of others becomes easily translated into a sense of threat, a fear hindering our own sense of appreciating what we have.

5. Robert Thurman, *Inner Revolution* (New York: Riverhead, 1998), 76.

Craving Style

Through consumption, grasping generates both the safety of identity as well as the thrill of becoming anew. As I consume, my sense of identity becomes tightly knit to my feeling states. "Shopping is a way that we search for ourselves and our place in the world," psychologist April Benson argues; "a lot of people conflate the search for self with the search for stuff." As I wear sophisticated Japanese designer clothes, my whole cognition speaks to me as if I am a sophisticated person. I want to feel like a queen or king again, and I crave more. As what I acquire arouses me, I am also seduced into believing I am what I consume.

The mantra of consumerism is *I crave; therefore I am*.

Perhaps we can find ways to deal with our cravings for the new, for the latest kick of dressed affirmation? A first step may be to start relating *to fashion*, rather than *from fashion*; to grow a sense of self-knowledge *with* fashion. When we are not paying attention, we let our cravings motivate our actions, whether we like it or not. By paying better attention to our emotions, we can better unpack what fashion does to us and how to respond to these emotions in a more wise way.

Even after the Buddha's victory, Mara did not disappear. Instead, Mara continued to live with the Buddha, kept returning with new temptations and doubts. In some traditions the demon eventually becomes a disciple of the Buddha. A possible task is to make friends with our desires, our self, at the most profound level possible. The task is not to resist or deny our experiences, but willingly invite Mara. In the moment of burning desire, and with this clearly recognizing the reality of craving, we may try to open a dialogue of understanding with Mara, examining the roots of our temptations to overcome Mara's intimidation.

A Clothing Diary

We seek pleasure and avoid pain. We connect pleasure with safety and happiness and think pain automatically translates to unhappiness. But craving is more easily dealt with if we learn to separate pleasure from happiness. Pleasure may often be aligned with desire and the play with anticipation; for example, in motion and striving toward a goal. Happiness can be a more passive contentment. The tension sought in pleasure is easily a victim to craving and grasping. Look carefully through your wardrobe. The fate of desire, more than happiness, is often on display there. Most wardrobes consist of stocked-up anticipation—yet unfulfilled dreams—as much as exhausted desires.

Start to think differently. Your wardrobe is not what garments you own, but what you experience when wearing garments. To pay more attention to these experiences, create yourself a clothing diary. Notice your feeling tones with an outfit over a day. When, and how, do you notice the way you are dressed? What does it feel like? What kind of attention would you want from that look? From whom? Pay attention to how your mind works in clothes, and it can guide you to a better understanding of why you dress in what garments, what you seek, and how to act more skillfully in relation to these emotions.

INTERVIEW

OTTO VON BUSCH: In the stories of Buddha's journey toward enlightenment, Mara is the demon that tempted Buddha. As I understood it, Buddha's response was not to ignore or neglect Mara, but acknowledge that desire is always present, recognize it, and overcome it. Could we say that fashion is one of today's tempting demons? What would be a wise way to challenge this temptation, especially today when fashion is so ubiquitous and seems to seep into all aspects of life?

JOSH KORDA: While Mara is referred to as a demon in the Suttas, it is understood by Buddhists to be an externalization of the Buddha's unskillful, materialist desires to find happiness and sensual pleasure in the consumable world, as opposed to spiritual practice. These materialist, easy-way-out cravings cropped up even after enlightenment. The Buddha would generally respond to these thoughts by saying the equivalent of "I see you, Mara," acknowledging but not acting on, rather than beating away or running from, his inner cravings.

Absolutely, fashion can certainly be produced and consumed in an attempt to find lasting happiness and peace of mind; producing and consuming is not the realm of lasting peace, though, and when done in moderation has its role in day-to-day life. Fashion, to my mind, is invariably interwoven with branding, the practice of implanting a unique identity and image for products in consumers' thoughts. Buddhist practice is to simply relate to a product in terms of its requisite function, not its identity in relation to other products. Giving an identity to a product is delusion.

OVB: The world is in motion; things change and so do our desires. Many argue that things change faster today than before, and that may be especially true in the realm of fashion, where collections in some stores change every week or even more often. Why do you think we are so interested and drawn to the new?

JK: Consumer appetites are virtually unappeasable, whether the hunger is for recurrent sales events or for "newness" in the form of monthly deliveries of fresh products. I gather that it's common for apparel items to stay on a sales floor for only a few months before they are marked down and quickly passed on to third-party resellers; rack space is constantly in demand.

At the heart of this "thirst for the new" is certainly what is commonly referred to as the "dopamine reward system" (or mesolimbic pathway in clinical terms), which lies at the heart of addictive craving. Simply put, the significant brain regions involved with pleasure and reward, such as the nucleus accumbens and ventral tegmental, release dopamine—feelings of power and invulnerability—as we hunt or shop for the new. Humorously, I've read that the fMRI brain scan of someone shopping online for clothes looks virtually identical to that of the cocaine addict. No doubt, tens of thousands of years ago, spotting a new tool made all the difference in our forebears' chances of survival. Newness holds the promise of survival advantage, even if it's "man leggings" or emoticon imagery on accessories.

Alas, the rewards of dopamine are all too brief and leave us hoping to acquire more, creating what we Buddhists might call a "samsaric" cycle of dissatisfaction. Certainly the Buddha noted that the "beautiful and new" (*subha*) was a convenient distraction that kept us from perceiving deeper, more-important considerations: the impermanence of life; the surety of old age, sickness, and death; and separation from the loved. The beautiful and new keeps us entranced; meanwhile, societal practice is to conceal the old in assisted-living facilities, the sick in hospitals, the dying in hospices, and so forth . . . reflecting on the fragility of the human condition is the great "craving suppressant" for consumers; few feel the urge to consume while reflecting actively on death and impermanence.

So the Buddha took time to urge his practitioners, including his son Rahula, to avoid fixating on the "beautiful and new" (*subha*) and to "meditate on the foul," that which is old and decaying; even dead bodies (Rahula Sutta, sn 2.11).

OVB: As fashion changes fast and so many of our peers keep up with the latest styles, not following fashion easily makes you feel old and foul. In social relations, especially in today's mobile, unstable, and highly competitive world, fashion thrives on our status anxiety. Rivals surround us, and many "arm" themselves with goods to enhance qualities that are socially recognized as attractive or prestigious. Even if it is not a fear for our life, it is a fear to our social position, to recognition, appreciation, and sense of self-worth. How are we to relate to this kind of fear?

JK: I suspect that we often use clothing as a way to protect our traumatic histories, to keep ourselves from being rewounded. Heterosexual men wear sports team jerseys not only to proclaim their allegiance to the club, but also as a way to "protect their masculinity." In early schoolyard experiences, boys taunt other boys over their masculinity, threatening physical abuse and social banishment if boys don't prove their strength, prowess, machismo. And so, from this point on, boys grow into men who secretly fear their "manhood" being questioned, and protect it by wearing a hockey jersey.

People who don't "fit" into the bland and predictable gender expectations can find themselves expelled from dominant groups in schools and other institutions. To be banished is traumatic; we are social beings, and any form of exclusion activates feelings of fear and vulnerability. Perhaps those who have been "evicted from the dominant heteronormative club" may both

- adapt fashion as a social marker to connect with other people who've been expelled, since feeling securely attached is essential for mental health

- use fashion as a way to protect themselves from being wounded again; by overtly acknowledging difference, we can say, "See, I'm not trying to be a member of your idiotic club anyway."

I feel a personal connection to these strategies, as, having had numerous threatening encounters with jocks and thugs in the late 1970s, I gravitated toward punk attire when I was a teen as a way to connect with other members of the subculture and to state my distaste for the dominant culture.

OVB: As you're saying, conceptual formations such as beauty (or "manhood," "womanhood," or "personhood"), coolness, or authenticity are all acting on us socially. They become excuses for taunting those who divert from or contest these ideals and demarcations.

Likewise, fashion may, as you say, act as an armor, to protect, or to say "I don't care." But an armor acknowledges one is a target, and may thus also expose a chink in the armor. Rivals may use it against each other. How should we understand the vulnerability of the "self" produced by consumerism or fashion?

JK: I would argue that the vulnerable self is not produced by consumerism but is produced by shaming, rejecting, or abusive relational experiences. We are social beings; we survive and thrive because we connect well, through language (left hemisphere) and emotions (right hemisphere). Vulnerability, as with all negative affects, is produced by disconnections.

onions

The sense of self is a recent event in evolution and would have appeared only if it provided a survival advantage—which it does: it provides us with a profoundly useful way to connect securely with others. What I mean is that a sense of self doesn't exist to differentiate ourselves from others, but rather it is an assemblage of markers, or dominant attributes (for example, "I am artsy" or "I am an intellectual"), which are employed to locate other people who share the same attributes—the intellectuals seek the intellectuals, the punks seek the punks, and so forth. For example, my teenage self, a young punk who grew up with a violent, alcoholic father, was constructed of self-beliefs—antiauthoritarian, victimized, marginalized—that provided me with the "identity badge" that allowed me to connect with other punks.

It's interesting to note that the neural circuits—largely situated in the ventromedial prefrontal cortex (VMPfc)—that activate when we describe our "self" coincide with the same region that is influenced when we process what other people think about us. To put it another way, the same region that constructs my idea of "me" is what processes other people's thoughts about "me." So the self is more a product of social influence than it is a personal domain. So many of my identity views are in fact constructed by other people. . . . We could further surmise, as the cognitive psychologist Matthew Lieberman and others have, that from a neuropsychological perspective there is no such thing as a nonconformist, since the construction of the individual "self" is always a socially influenced process.

To bring this all back to fashion, I would suggest that it's a kind of external sign, or social message, advertising our core attributes and self-beliefs, in essence an advertisement of ourselves to others, which eventually provide a uniform that solidifies our membership within the tribe that provides us with protection. Until we have secured our membership, we may shift and change styles or explore different "looks" until our messages are received and we are securely connected.

OVB: Yes, consumerism supports us to build a self based on accessible goods, connecting to others with the acquisition of stuff, shopping together, displaying our new "hauls," using consumption as a form of shared entertainment. This is a type of self that is promoted through fashion, a self on the move, continuously becoming anew, updating itself visually, grasping onto acknowledgment. Does this approach to the self differ from other forms of building a self, based on the mastering of skills, like learning to play an instrument well?

JK: Indeed, there are many ways to construct a sense of self, or lasting, secure identity. A self based on the acquisition of apparel or other consumer goods might seem to be a shallow misrepresentation of identity, especially when contrasted with a self constructed from skills that have been slowly mastered over a period of years, such as artistry, craft, athletic prowess, and so on. And indeed, competence, dexterity, and ingenuity do display the mark of an individual more than simply purchasing an array of products; curating one's ensemble is a hallow endeavor when compared with leaving one's mark in a creative endeavor.

Yet, it's worth noting as well that all forms of self-construction, as the Buddha noted, can set oneself up for disappointment and deprivation, for skills that are mastered can erode. For example, the great pianist can develop arthritis; someone who designs and creates lovely, unique, one-of-a-kind quilts can lose their eyesight. In such cases, what happens to one's "self"? The dancer's fluidity of movement can be eroded with time. It might be tempting to create a self based on the cleverness of our thoughts, but even our reasoning can be stripped away in the processes of aging or mental illness.

So from another perspective, constructing a self from what one purchases is just another desperate grab for a feeling of solidity amid the fleeting, and if it provides those who feel marginalized with a supportive connection with others, membership in a clan, it might even have benefits that the isolated artist, working alone in studio, might find beneficial.

OVB: Fashion offers a sense of belonging: that one is part of a group, and distinct from another. It is like going to a concert and everyone dances to the same music: we are all apart, but in unity, moving in concert. This sense of unity, of being alone together, gives a strong sense of belonging. Is there also a neurological trait that also rewards us for joining the right group, or a feeling of unity?

JK: Absolutely. We are social animals; we didn't become the dominant species because we run particularly fast, dig holes, or climb trees with alacrity; we thrive because we can bond deeply with our families, friends, tribes; our brains have sophisticated systems that connect us with others. In the past, tribes composed of individuals willing to share their resources with each other would survive, while tribes composed of individuals that would jealously hoard their food and shelter would perish. Eventually we developed anterior cingulate cortexes that highlight not only physical pain and pleasure, but also the shame of social disconnection and pleasures of secure tribal membership. The hardwiring of the emotional brain compels us to inhibit selfish impulses at times, while urging us to consider what benefits our connection to others.

For example, we can mentalize meaning; we can read each other's emotions and discern, to a certain degree, each other's motivations, which allows us to sync our actions with one another. Even our deepest sense of self is linked to regions (namely, the ventromedial access) that are activated by what other people think of us. So our emotional activations, such as pride, shame, joy, remorse, and loneliness, are constantly interweaving with the basic impulses of fear and reward. Were it not for prosocializing emotions, we would spin only between fear and selfish pleasure hunting.

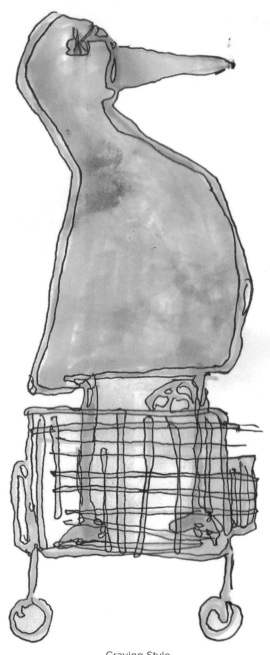

A Desire Diary

Ask yourself: Where is craving felt in your body and in your life? Often we confuse desire with such a simple thing as low blood sugar. I may feel a need to buy that garment, yet I never really made the conscious choice to buy it. I tell myself it just "happened" to be in my way. Mapping feeling tones and desires can help make sense of cause and effect when it comes to consumption choices. Attend closely to what is usually habitual and unconscious. How do I know I just "need" those new sneakers or pants? Be honest with yourself. Remember: you must be present to notice how emotions move your thoughts.

Create a desire diary—pay attention to the times and places you shop; is it after certain accomplishments? Or after conflicts with friends or a partner? Or in situations of uncertainty and confusion? Or to share experiences with friends? Notice the states of your mind: the attraction to some (which can be greed and lust), and the aversion from some expressions (including shame, disappointment, fear). But also notice your relation to how others dress; do you feel envy or jealousy toward some? Disgust and disdain toward others? Don't shy away: we are all emotionally connected to the world, and too often in a compulsive way. Without practice, we remain victims to these responses and keep shopping without really noticing.

WALL OF MASKS

CHAPTER 3

Addiction

In the Wheel of Life, the symbolic representation of cyclic existence prominent in Buddhism, there is a realm of Hungry Ghosts. Creatures with small mouths, narrow necks, and skeletal limbs inhabit it. Yet, malnourished as they are, the ghosts have large, bloated bellies. With thin necks they cannot swallow, so they remain endlessly hungry, fed only by their greed, envy, and jealousy.

This is the domain of addiction, obsession, and compulsion. Suffering from spiritual emptiness, we too constantly seek something outside ourselves, hungry for attachment. Insatiable, we yearn for fulfillment, or at least some relief. In this realm, the aching emptiness is perpetual since nothing can fully soothe the hunger for more.

If we cannot find a way to exit this realm, we will never know what we really need. We keep grasping selfhood with insatiable hunger. Like ghosts we haunt the fashion boutiques, yet our thirst for the new can never be satisfied. Craving consumes our entire life and turns into addiction.

With today's abundance of cheap fashion, the three poisons of greed, aversion, and delusion have seeped into the everyday mind of even those with modest means. With fast fashion and ubiquitous access to fashion media, the suffering of dissatisfaction bleeds into the mind of everyone; "I need that hit of desire again."

As soon as I feel low on energy or have a bad day, my attention is drawn to quick aesthetic sugar, a quick fix: without really thinking, I get into the fashion store on my way back home or browse the store apps in a tired haze at night, just a short click away from a purchase I soon forgot I did. With the numbing feeling of habit, my relation to fashion turns into "McFashion," as unsatisfying, commonplace, and utterly forgettable as the fast-food equivalent.[6] Our wardrobes become the thin necks of our hungry fashion ghosts, too small to fit all our ephemeral desires.

6. Michele Lee, *Fashion Victim: Our Love-Hate Relationship with Dressing, Shopping, and the Cost of Style* (New York: Broadway Books, 2003).

It is not uncommon to frame one's relation to fashion in terms of addiction. John Waters gives a great example of this in his book *Role Models*, when he encounters the cool crew dressed in Comme des Garcons:

> *Suddenly I felt like a drug addict who takes his first shot of heroin. I was about to become addicted to Comme des Garcons, and maybe, if I worked hard, Rei Kawakubo could be my dealer. I left the store feeling like a king.*

PEICG
PIECES OF YOU   LOOKING BACK AT YOU

Break the comfort of habit.

Addiction has a bad name; it is far too often moralized upon, which makes it harder to address in an unbiased way. But addiction is an extreme expression of what is otherwise normal behavior, if it is drinking, eating, working, or seeking other forms of pleasure and escape. It is important for recovery to see that life does not have to be unsatisfactory after opening up to deal with suffering emerging from addiction. That would be a bad strategy for confronting unskillful behavior. Instead, examine the habits, emotions, and compulsive thoughts that pull you toward unsatisfactory habits (e.g., late-night online shopping sprees).

Notice how addiction emerges from imbalance, not necessarily the substance of addiction itself. Spend the time catching up with your dressed self. List moments when you have shopped in blind habit, perhaps some online last-minute sale? Or to relieve the stress before an upcoming deadline? Far too often we dress under the same anxious stress as we live.

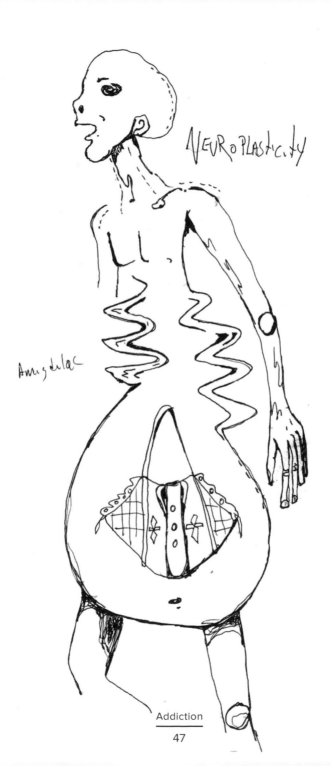

NEUROPLASTICITY

Amygdala

In the April 2013 issue of *GQ* magazine, author Buzz Bissinger confesses his addiction to shopping for expensive clothes in ways similar to that of Waters. In a glistening piece of writing, he divulges the rich, sensual experience of getting drawn into the Gucci orbit, spending very extensive sums of money on clothing, especially leather.

> *I have an addiction. It isn't drugs or gambling: I get to keep what I use after I use it. But there are similarities: the futile feeding of the bottomless beast and the unavoidable psychological implications, the immediate hit of the new that feels like an orgasm and the inevitable coming-down. . . . It has taken a while to figure out what works and what doesn't work, but Gucci men's clothing best represents who I want to be and have become—rocker, edgy, tight, bad boy, hip, stylish, flamboyant, unafraid.*

Bissinger is sitting front row at the Gucci Milan fashion week men's show, and his experience of the new collection takes him aback, his desire racing, overpowering the mind:

> *I see the collection, and the pheromones of hot clothing defeat the part of the brain that rations rationality . . . I have to have it. I don't have to have it. I need it. I don't need it. I can afford it. I can't afford it. It is the cycle familiar to anyone who fetishizes high fashion.*

As Bissinger notices, the experience of clothing can be something more than mere symbolism:

> *I wanted the power that sex provides, all eyes wanting to fuck you and you knowing it. . . . I love looking at myself in the mirror when I buy something new. I love the sexual rush to the degree that I wonder if it has become a replacement for actual sex. But just like fucking, the magic of new clothing wears off quickly, and you can't resist the cravings for new purchases.*

What Bissinger highlights is that fashion is a toxicant. The experience of fashion that Bissinger describes is a rush soaked in the poisons of greed, aversion, and delusion. These three components are immensely powerful forces in human life. They are also core elements that make fashion so successful and essential in today's social life. It is an addictive rush of affirmation, and it fuels a sense of achievement, the agency of catching people's attention, the rush of being seen with eyes of desire.

We crave fashion because it satisfies so much more than mere hunger: it taps into our social cognition as we compare ourselves to our peers. Fashion loves to play with social transgressions and metamorphosis, in one moment turning master into slave, and the next, slave into master. It is like the model and judge Heidi Klum famously says in the TV show *Project Runway*: "In fashion, one day you're in, and the next day you're out."

But even if we usually think so, addiction is not something that merely affects the subject, the addict. Addiction has social consequences and tears through the social fabric. Because it produces as well as relieves anxiety, it also has viral properties that affect others. Happiness may be contagious, but so is violence. Not only may the passions or social moods spread like germs, but the addict starts treating others as mere instruments to fuel the reward cycle, making others invisible, superfluous, or even disposable.

Does fashion make us treat others in a similar way, as mere mirrors of our own desire to be seen, thus making us crave for ever more fashion and covet our gilded chains? We remain unable to express our own emotions and vulnerabilities, yet fashion offers a safe screen from behind which one can judge others. Behind the "shallowness" of fashion, we can laugh at the flaws of celebrities in the paparazzi magazines and gossip about peers without any guilt.

Behind fashion, our peers become screens onto which we project our own powerlessness and insecurity with a certain sense of nastiness.

Because, after all, it's "just" fashion, isn't it?

INTERVIEW

OTTO VON BUSCH: These days, words that before seemed to signal various forms of personal challenges and problems have entered everyday slang concerning fashion and consumption, and it is not uncommon to hear of "retail therapy" or "shopping addiction." This may of course be just a play on words, but it may also signal how we today turn to fashion and consumption for some very basic human needs. This may be especially tempting in today's "fast fashion," when clothes can be as cheap as a coffee or other forms of easy leisure.

Many of us use fashion consumption to deal with our emotions, getting ready for a party, date, or job interview, as well as dealing with the emotions afterward, to "move on." Similarly, we use fashion as we seek social affirmation and the feeling of control we crave, and there is often a social pressure to keep up. Perhaps we need to start our discussion at the very basics: What is addiction, how do we recognize it, and how do you usually address it?

JOSH KORDA: In my view, addiction is an attempt to sidestep the vulnerability of establishing open, authentic, empathetic connections with other people.

Human beings are social beings. Our survival advantage doesn't accrue from running fast, digging holes, or scampering up trees; we don't have shells that can protect us. But what we do well is connect to others, and in multiple ways. We can bond through language, telling stories about ourselves and sharing plans, or through the emotional displays of facial expressions, laughter and tears, body language, tones of voice. When I convey my frustrations through nonverbal means, and you empathize by reflecting that back through looks of concern or appreciation, we connect on a much-deeper level than language, and you help me "normalize" or "process" my emotions.

When we experience difficult emotions, part of the process of being with that emotion is being able to express it to other people safely—without fear that they'll reject, shame, or criticize us. We all need this process to "handle" our emotions; without it, our emotional activations become increasingly unstable, unmanageable, turbulent. (Note how quickly most adults, when imprisoned in solitary confinement, will experience psychosis.)

Of course, many of us grow up in family systems that fail to provide reliably tolerant emotion regulation. Or, during our socializing years in schools, we are traumatized by bullying or institutional shaming; peers mock our vulnerability, our awkwardness, our authentic expressions of feelings. When this occurs we lose faith that other people can be relied upon to help us process certain emotions—our loneliness, frustration, sadness, anger, and so forth. So we'll seek behaviors or substances that numb these effects, seeking to regulate emotions without relying on other people. Unfortunately, addictive behaviors and substances alleviate emotions only briefly, through suppression, rather than through empathetic interpersonal connection, which is lasting.

Addiction, from my perspective, always leads to disconnection. It ingrains the belief that we can't safely express certain emotions. Retail therapy—the swipe of the credit card—temporarily relieves feelings of powerlessness and lack of fulfillment.

OVB: As you mentioned earlier, there is a neurological pleasure in shopping, even similar to that of taking drugs. In this kind of pleasure hunting, it sometimes feels we are triggered by the pursuit of goods—the sensation of wanting something, and sometimes the expectations of the coming pleasure. Sometimes the acquisition, what reasonably should be the climax, only delivers a feeling of exhaustion. How does the excitement of the hunt relate to the pleasure of accomplishment?

JK: Our brains synthesize and expend dopamine to operate; along with glutamate, it's an essential neurotransmitter that supports voluntary movement, sustained cognition, the desire to attain survival advantages, working memory, the ability to learn, and much more. Dopamine is the fuel that charges the neural circuits that create the urge to acquire things; these are the circuits (ventral tegmental area, striatum, etc.) that result in impulsive urges to consume goods, drugs, food, sex, and all other addictive behaviors.

To varying degrees, all brains have circuits that regulate dopamine, hopefully at levels that don't result in addictive behavioral patterns. But, of course, many brains have shortfalls in dopamine regulation; as levels increase, so do compulsive acts.

As your question notes, while dopamine is referred to as a "reward" neurotransmitter, it is principally released during the hunt for goods and diminishes quickly once we actually achieve our goal; dopamine is a pleasurable sensation that easily masks ambient feelings of anxiety, boredom, sadness. So it's quite natural to prefer online shopping over feeling lonely; looking at hundreds of images of shoes on an e-commerce website releases dopamine throughout the search, but once we click the "buy" button the dopamine charge diminishes and any negative, underlying feelings masked by the dopamine release reemerge to consciousness.

TRY IT

You'll like It

This is the behavioral loop beneath all addiction:

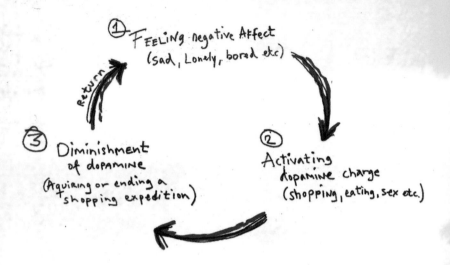

At heart, our addictive cycles are not about the objects (shoes, apparel, food) we acquire, but an unconscious desire to conceal negative feelings from awareness.

I'd like to note here that the Buddhist dharma separated *tanha*, which we know as the dopamine-fueled charge to accumulate, from *upadana*, the stressful, less pleasurable states that follow, which involve clinging to our pleasures, living amid thoughts of self and others. So the distinction between the single-minded pleasure of wanting versus the diminished unquiet of owning was made. Roughly 2,500 years ago, when the Buddha noted the universal role of craving in suffering, the cycle of addiction was in full flourish.

The solution, of course, is to learn how to tolerate and process the negative feelings we conceal by shopping, so that the addictive fire that drives us to consume will be discharged. The original role of mindfulness, or *sati*, was to meet this requirement for mental health: it shows us how to create a safe container for negative feelings and mind states.

Once we learn how to tolerate negative effects, it doesn't mean we'll stop purchasing goods altogether, since the Buddha noted that human beings have requisites necessary to survive — enough clothing to keep us warm, food to sustain activity, means to communicate — but hopes it will result in behavior that isn't bound by reckless consumption, the kind that needlessly depletes both natural resources and personal bank accounts.

OVB: Much design is about gently nudging consumers into the pleasure of consumption. So it is quite easy to see how we get "hooked" on the dopamine charge of shopping. I guess it also happens to everyday routines such as checking for likes on Facebook and such: they are, after all, systems designed to seek our attention and offer micro-rewards. In a similar vein, shopping is staged to be like a hunt, with pop-up stores, limited editions, etc., a form of continual cycle of excitement and boredom. Does this neurological priming for the hunt relate to other forms of entertainment, such as gambling? Can the brain get bored with its own reward opiates, those that are released, for example, by anticipation, thrill, risk, or fulfillment?

JK: Absolutely; drugs that imitate the effect of dopamine on the brain (for example, those that treat Parkinson's disease and restless-leg syndrome) are well known to trigger gambling, compulsive sexual appetites, and shopping, which is not surprising since they involve the same striatal neural pathways.

As for "getting bored with its own reward opiates," I'd slightly change the focus: the brain doesn't get tired of dopamine, but it gets used to the sensations and experiences that activate dopamine (i.e., we don't get tired of feeling great; we get tired of the things that make us feel great). This is referred to as "desensitization" and "habituation," in essence the diminishing responsiveness of the brain to the external conditions that trigger pleasurable feelings. . . . Desensitization can lead to compulsive food bingeing, as one experiencing diminishing rewards will consume more and more to get the same level of satisfaction. Generally speaking, in the absence of neural imbalance, the root cause of desensitization is overconsumption: we consume too much of a good thing. Over the years, people have to purchase more apparel, take greater business risks, watch more porn, or take more cocaine to get the same buzz, as it were.

This is one of the fundamental flaws of basing our pursuit of happiness on career ambitions, sex, or consumerism: dopamine rewards are short lived and increasingly challenging to activate; meanwhile, serotonin, the neurotransmitter at the heart of well-being and contentment, doesn't appear in thrilling rollercoaster rides. It rises in long, smooth, gradual inclines; it takes its time to appear and disappear, which is why serotonin-based drugs (SSRIs) can take weeks to kick in; the brain doesn't habituate to the external cues that produce serotonin — most reliably, connecting securely with other people. In short, lasting peace of mind is more likely to be found in the gradual rewards of friendship and volunteerism than acquisition or attainment.

OVB: As I see it, fashion endorses a binge/purge behavior, especially today, with a surplus of cheap and accessible fashion. Those with a habit of shopping for cheap clothes need to get rid of their surplus, the average wardrobes being simply too small. That is why so many brands discuss "sustainability" today; the system suffers from fashion bulimia: with anticipation, fulfillment, waste, and start again. Are there also addictive behaviors connected to binge/purge patterns?

JK: Yes, but let's take a step back and start at another end — as we are beings weighed down with an existential awareness of our own vulnerability, living toward the looming inevitability of death, it's natural to seek some form of rescue from the inevitable: aging, sickness, and loss. In other words, we hope to ward off the despairing thoughts through our efforts to establish an exemption.

Our brands come to the rescue. We brand ourselves to stand out from the "crowd." The crowd, after all, is those other people who will grow old, feel pain, die, and be quickly forgotten: the walking shadows, strutting and fretting their hour upon the stage, then heard no more. So the "great escape" is to get everyone looking at us, to stay in the center stage, caught in the spotlight of the world, to be seen as powerful. The dopamine rush of attention makes us feel invulnerable.

And yet we are also social animals, deeply conformist. Alone in the wild we perish — we've prospered due to our twin frontal lobes, which allow us to connect in so many ways: language, facial expressions, body language, and a variety of cultural signs, or brands. It's hard written into our neural networks to do anything, to please and conform to win admittance into a pack. In addition to behavioral imitation, we use brands toward this aim.

So identity expressed through mass-manufactured brands is the perfect example of the human condition: we seek the perfect identity to win connection; we want other people to see and affirm us, to reinforce our existence through admiration.

Brands bring us such attention, which makes us feel solid, substantial, loved, even though the act of purchasing and wearing requires little bravery, heroism, inspiration, or insight. A brand simply announces we belong to a tribe, a tribe that we'd like to believe is important and memorable.

While I may connect, on an unconscious level, with other guys who wear Dickies pants or Carhartt caps, it also plays into an underlying desire—born of the anxiety that my life doesn't matter—that I am smarter than the next fellow, who doesn't wear Dickies.

But to come to your question: The binge-and-purge pattern can be seen in different lights. One obvious perspective lies in our feelings of powerlessness, shame, and social isolation. Essentially we consume for the "I feel amazing" dopamine rewards, all providing the experience of power and invulnerability. Eventually feelings of guilt or remorse set in, for when we overconsume we worry that we'll be seen by others as indulgent and lacking control. So we purge; throw out or expel the evidence. Of course, the shame that arises in the wake of bingeing can activate despondency, which creates the conditions for future binges; in essence a "samsaric" cycle is established.

OVB: Are there several types or expressions of addiction that could be relevant in the realm of fashion? One type, as you mentioned, is the addiction to shopping as compensation for experiences of rejection and abandonment. But could there also be other types, where we become dependent on the approval of others, our own ego so weak we cannot fully exist without being affirmed by others, and thus reliant to the verification of their demands, even if these can turn into abusive relations, such as bullying?

JK: A healthy dependence doesn't involve accomplishing anything; it's a mutual recognition of the human condition — all humans are social beings seeking to be deeply seen in the eyes of a tolerant "other," based on a disclosure of nonverbal feelings. The deal of mutuality is sealed when our emotions are mirrored back to us through the kind facial expressions and gestures of the other (friend, caretaker, lover, therapist, teacher).

Deeper bonding requires the strength to be vulnerable, since we've all experienced early interpersonal wounds that occurred during disclosing our impulses and desires to intolerant peers and family members. So while we all seek the substantial, meaningful interactions between friends, based on mutual recognition of feelings, we can also greatly recoil from the attendant vulnerability and risk of shaming or rejection.

Fashion can provide a subterfuge, a way to convey feelings of uniqueness, outsider status, creativity, sexual impulses, and political leanings. Though the messages are expressed, they're expressed via trends, accessories, subcultures, brand allegiance, etc. Perhaps fashion can be seen as a kind of communication, a language that expresses, indirectly, elements of the "true" spontaneous self, even though the iterations are purchased off the rack. When we are brave, we don't dress for success; we dress to express — much as the dandies and neoromantics used clothing to shout the love that dares not speak its name . . .

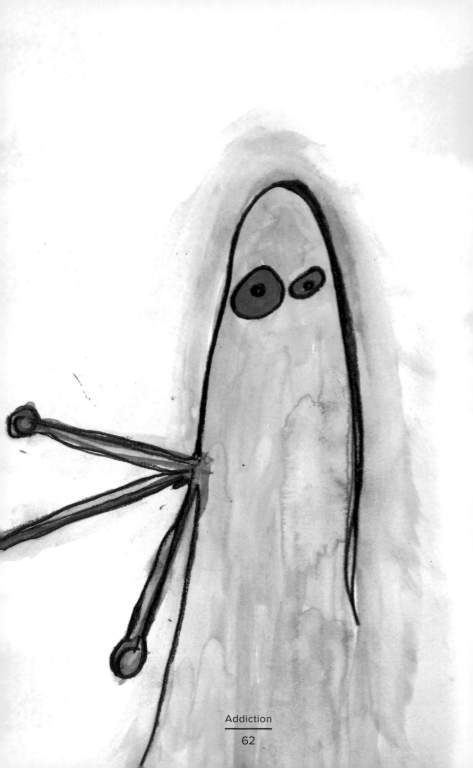

Notice unsatisfactory habits.

Habit is familiarity, the safety that comes with routines, even if we know they have adversarial influence on our health or even happiness. Far too often, we seek comfort in behavior that actually makes us unhappy—like looking too often in the mirror, even on a bad hair day. We stay with the familiar, even if it brings suffering. We often seek comfort in reasoning that accepts and legitimizes our own suffering— the delusion of knowledge helps explain why we get what we "deserve."

Challenge the comfort of unhealthy habits. Instead, practice with gratitude, since it increases our appreciation for what we have. It helps us become more aware of what moves us, and find balance. With attention and acceptance we can start unpacking how to change. Stop to reflect on habits that bring suffering, judgment, and anxiety. Challenge them by making a list of what you are grateful for, moments where you are at peace. At what moments do you feel comfort, in private as well as public? Look carefully: Can you draw parallels between your dress and emotions at these moments?

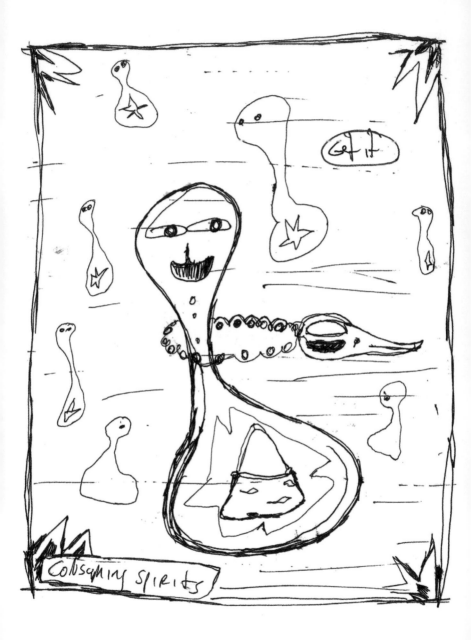

CHAPTER 4

Recovery

Samsara is the Sanskrit term for the wandering and suffering-laden cyclic change of all matter, life, and existence. On our samsaric journey we roam through the Wheel of Life, from one realm to the other. Almost all of us come through the realms of Hungry Ghosts, or even ending up in the flaming pits of hell from time to time.

It is a hard journey, full of disappointments, but it is not hopeless. In each of the six realms in the wheel of life there is a Bodhisattva, an enlightened being that aspires to save all beings from suffering. There is a Bodhisattva in the realm of the gods, one with the demigods, one with the humans, one among hungry ghosts, and another with the animals, and finally one in hell.

So also in the smoking sulfur of eternal suffering, there is a guide to soothe travelers' journeys.

The Bodhisattva of hell is Ksitigarbha (Dizang in China, Jizo in Japan). Especially prominent and easily recognizable in Japanese culture, he cares for lost children; protects the souls of aborted, stillborn, or miscarried babies; and, in depictions, often shields babies with his robes. Jizo statues in Japan are often dressed and adorned by devotees, and some make clothes for the small figures of Jizo at the local shrines. Along the roads in East Asia it is not uncommon to see small statues of a Bodhisattva at the intersection of roads, helping a traveler to chose the correct path in life.

The presence of Bodhisattvas in every realm suggests there is hope of enlightenment in each one of them. But it also highlights that we are not staying safe in any one place but continually cross between them as we are reborn, or within lifetimes. We may temporarily recover from the realm of hungry ghosts to the realm of humans or even gods, yet we are always at risk of relapse back to a lower stage. Nothing is permanent and change is inevitable; this is the doom of samsara. At a crisis or intersection in life, we may temporarily lose hold, fall, and return to an undesirable state. Yet, with enough presence we may still save the situation and chose the better path.

Fashion is a continual cycle of change where nothing is permanent: each new collection a fork in the path, a new necessary choice. In the ecstasy of a successful shopping spree, we may assure ourselves that we will keep these new goods for a long time, yet with only a bit of experience we know such promises are futile. Change is inflicted upon us; we cannot choose what is in fashion.

With fashion, change is made attractive. Even if we are trapped downstream, there is an allure to newness, to the promise of seductive change. Each moment, or new season, offers a new beginning. It gives room for a fresh start, to progress, excel, and soar over our peers. But just like we may ask where our clothes are produced, we should perhaps be asking *where* our desires to continually remodel the self comes from, what it is we strive to leave behind: to understand our mind's Wanderlust. Our cravings, attachments, habits, and emotions emerge from somewhere, and to see our path forward, we need to be aware of where we came from.

Buddhist teacher Pema Chödrön frames attachment as an urge with a "sticky feeling" tacked like glue to our insecurity, unease, and restlessness. It manifests in anxiety and habitual twitches toward security; to peeking toward the phone, just another drink, an impulsive purchase.

The momentum behind the urge or craving is so strong that we never pull out of the habitual pattern of turning to poison for comfort.

It does not necessarily have to involve a substance or a particular thing; it can be saying thoughtless words or approaching everything with a comparing mind. That is a major hook. Something triggers an old pattern we would rather not feel, and we tighten up and hook into comparing or criticizing. This gives us a puffed-up satisfaction and a feeling of control that provides short-term relief from uneasiness.[7]

The habit of fashion consumption can be a similar hook. In a wounded moment, or just to fill some time to spare, I start browsing the stores, looking for a bargain to keep my mind in a pleasant mode of business. I hardly even notice my craving. Or a hook emerges as a possibility; a new job or partner, a change in life, and what started as a temporary surge of pleasure quickly fades into unease and reshapes into craving and new habitual hunger. With frustration, craving turns into habit; the same set of patterns of responses, ignoring other ways of dealing with life experiences. Self-contained, intoxicated with the safety of the self, the mind is reduced to the self-hypnosis of automatic call and response.

Like ambition, fashion easily imprisons us within the walls that define success. The euphoric kick that comes with being admired easily turns into new hunger for being seen; just another quick purchase and the sticky hook is back, luring the mind deeper into the snares of samsara.

It is an uphill struggle. Most of us probably spend more time looking in the mirror during an average week than turning our attention to what is really going on inside us. And even if we try spiritual practice, it is hard to balance an hour of meditation or contemplation a week with the average of thirty or more hours we spend turning our attention to media and our phones. And as Buddhist teacher Chögyam Trungpa warns, we easily grasp after material accomplishment even within the context of spiritual pursuit, accumulating the symbols of wisdom around the self, rather than breaking free. Seated on expensive and authentic meditation pillows, we wear the number of blissful retreats like shining pearls on our chokers.

7. Pema Chödrön, "How we get hooked, how we get unhooked," in *Hooked!: Buddhist Writings on Greed, Desire, and the Urge to Consume*, ed. Stephanie Keza (Boston: Shambhala, 2005), 28.

Try to embrace risk.

Stepping out of habits that have emerged from fear is hard, and the new freedom can be petrifying. If we have been in a state of "fearing" (clinging to the safety of bondage) too long, even our anxiety feels like good company, protective as it is. But fear is natural and a healthy emotion when seen and acknowledged. In small steps, embrace the freedom that comes with risk and anticipation. With practice, mitigate the process that links risk with fearing and the habitual escape to bondage. Don't withdraw from risk or escape from its freedom, but spend time practicing with anticipation.

Get lost a bit, try to be open to discomfort, be merciful to this sense of exposure. Then find your way home again; see yourself from a new angle. Use your next moment in a store to try something radically new. Test things and reflect; what could be the worst thing to happen? What could be the best thing? Surrender to the moment of risk; allow it to show you a new path. What changes in life would you desire, and could your engagement with clothes somehow be part of this new path? Remember: don't be foolish. Courage is not about denying or overcoming fear, but understanding and acting wisely with fear. Write down your experiences.

A transition toward processes of awareness does not happen overnight. And with a consumerist mindset, the risk is that a new emerging self-understanding acts as a new form of self-centered spiritual materialism. New judgment, painted in spiritual colors, may emerge that still keeps reproducing the same ideals of slim Caucasian bodies we meet in fashion as well as on the covers of the yoga magazines — milking existing power structures for benefit or maintaining the status quo.

Yet, the answer is not to denounce fashion — it is everywhere, and its corresponding judgments seep into our cognition and being whether we want it or not. But we can pay attention to these processes and become aware of our judgments. Enjoy the pleasures and affirming energies fashion brings, but stay awake and try to reach the roots of desire. Be aware of its impermanence and the traps of craving, and cultivate a wider sense of aesthetic agency. Play with the pleasures of fashion with open eyes; don't let it poison your mind. As the Buddha said to a rich man asking about a wise relationship to money, it is not wealth and power that enslave the mind, but the clinging to wealth and power.

It is not enough to practice mindfulness about a socially produced poison; it must also be addressed socially.

In a similar vein, critics argue that Buddhism only creates conditions for kinder and gentler suffering and does not alleviate the pain and violence of an unjust world. But a Buddhist perspective helps unveil the causes of suffering, not only individually but also on a systemic or structural level. It is not about submission to the violence of the world, but untangling its roots, starving what feeds competitive greed, rivalries, violence, and fear. It is about tracing the roots of individual as well as societal suffering to better know how to displace violence and addiction and start a healing process.

We can have a wiser relationship to fashion, turning from a habitual reflex of immediately figuring out how to most quickly *acquire* it, to shift toward a mindset to instinctively think how to go about *staying with it*. It is not about rejecting desire, but bringing it to awareness, feeling it, modulating it, and also being present enough to actually enjoy and persist *in the pleasure of desire* rather than moving too quickly toward easily forgettable satisfaction. And we must practice to do so beyond buying new stuff. Liberation means to give up the need to dominate and control, not only to break free. It means to escape the traps of unskilled behaviors. Liberation is about locating ourselves within our experiences and overcoming the fear of getting involved with the messy emotions we engage with through fashion. To see where our sticky hooks come from in order to make wiser choices on our path.

Reflecting on fashion is about playing with desires, but it is a play that also asks us, *What are you rejecting or trying to escape? What roots of your emotions are you unwilling to accept?*

Fashion can be a way of *being with* suffering, allowing confusion to seep in, and staying with the discomfort long enough to untangle its roots.

Disappointments can be great teaching moments, since they point us toward the formation of expectations and who defines our notion of success.

We need to practice with the cravings for affirmation, status, and novelty, practice with the feeling tones of desire. Go to the front lines, where the action is, where the risk is. We only learn little staying behind leaders. Be comforted that there is a Bodhisattva even in hell, so there's probably one also in fashion. Allow yourself to practice. As the hook catches your desires, stop for a moment and really *feel fashion*.

HOW TO BUILD A FORT

1. GET SOME MATERIALS

~~3.~~ 2. BUILD IT

3. HOPE SOME ASSHOLE DOESNT RIP IT DOWN.

INTERVIEW

OTTO VON BUSCH: Can some forms of addiction produce positive opportunities? By this I mean that an addiction may become a signal that helps us see some deeper currents in our life that we need to deal with, that we can no longer run away from. How can finding oneself in addiction be turned into something better, reconciliation and wisdom?

JOSH KORDA: Well, an addiction is, by my definition, an attempt to use substances or behaviors to replace the necessary open and honest interpersonal connections requisite for regulating our emotions and impulses. In other words, to process our feelings without suppression or harmful loss of control, we need to express them to others who — through attentiveness, mirroring facial expressions, tone of voice, and gestures — help pacify our agitations, loneliness, sorrows, and so forth.

The ability to process our emotions starts early in life; it's developed in the original relationships with those who were essential to our survival, our primary caretakers. To develop self-regulation demands nonverbal connection; if our needs for connection led to disappointment, we'll struggle to trust others and seek addictive replacements.

Yes, it could indeed be argued that addiction is akin to the "canary in the mine shaft," letting us know that underlying trust and attachment issues require our attention. So be it; I've heard some members of Alcoholics Anonymous express their "gratitude for being an alcoholic" since they doubt they'd find the willingness or determination to express their feelings without bottoming out in addiction.

Additionally, some have suggested that addictive mind states can lead some individuals to develop highly honed skills. Think of the thirteen-year-old boy who struggles to make friends in school, so he spends untold hours a day alone, practicing the piano and bass guitar, hoping to sidestep the vulnerable stages of making friends by winning adulation for his musicianship (this is a portrait of myself, some forty years ago).

Is the time spent developing skills to replace interpersonal intimacy worth it? People who enjoy the work of talented artists who honed their crafts as the byproduct of addiction may believe so. But the artists themselves rarely find much peace of mind and often fall into less attractive forms of addiction: alcoholism, drugs, shopping, sex, food. Not a good trade.

OVB: So to deal with addiction means to figure out a path out of it. The idea of "recovery" gives the impression that I recover to the state before addiction. But, paradoxically, that was also the state that produced addiction in the first place. Can I recover to get forward, not as "before" (a before that created addiction), but toward something else, a more wise and healthy place?

JK: Indeed, many people in recovery make the same point: most of us have nothing good to recover—we started out life in unsuccessful relationships; there were no halcyon days.

Some believe they had wonderful childhoods, but interviews with grown adults who during their childhoods were observed by psychologists to have poor attachments demonstrate that it's quite common for those with disorganized attachment to believe in false versions of their own childhoods, for we can paint over our darkest pain with bright, rosy colors.

So yes, "recovery" should actually be a word that suggests growth and cultivation, not return.

OVB: So let's go for healing for now in the sense of growth. How will we go about healing to help us move forward but also deal with the damage done?

JK: Adults with attachment issues—which lie at the heart of most psychological disorders—can, in a healthy, interpersonal environment, connect with the feelings associated with early losses and process the early caretaking bonds that didn't occur. In one-on-one work with a therapist or Buddhist teacher, or attending support group meetings, individuals can learn how to develop secure attachments; eventually the old definitions of love—etched amid the original abandonments and misconnections of childhood—are rewritten by the new interactions—supportive, tolerant, mirroring. It's worth the effort.

OVB: Is this how we could sum up a more "wise" relationship to fashion?

JK: The key to achieving peace of mind in an industry such as fashion is practicing kindness, compassion, and equanimity toward one's coworkers, practicing generosity and virtue (refusing to speak harmfully), staying mindful in noting and relaxing the underlying stresses that accumulate in the body and mind, and focusing one's efforts outside work toward endeavors that develop unconditional peace (meditation and service, for example).

OVB: So perhaps we need to redefine "retail therapy" into a therapy that deals with recovering from retail, rather than using retail as a substitute for dealing with the issues at hand. Perhaps designers could think about how to help produce mutual security, where users feel safe to grow, rather than keep on arming fashionistas with new outfits in a perpetual style war?

So if we would generalize about shopping addiction or fashion, could you speculate about what would be a good way to start dealing with one's addiction to continually buying new clothes?

JK: I would certainly suggest observing, without judgment, the internal experiences that occur right before and during the craving to shop. What do we feel in the body (which muscle groups are tense and contracted)? What emotional states are experienced (for example, loneliness, anger, sadness, fear, excitement, confusion, self-doubt)? Does our attention and awareness feel small and contracted, or jumpy and anxious, or expansive? And the thoughts that urge us to shop, are they simply repetitive or demeaning, or grandiose, or fearful?

Addictions are attempts to regulate, or protect us from internal states; in essence we drink, snort, shoot up, binge on food, cut ourselves, and shop to avoid feeling internal states, especially painful gut feelings. As we see how addiction is an attempt to distract or divert our attention from inner feelings, we can practice feeling and talking about those states, or we can develop more-useful practices to alleviate our loneliness, sadness, etc.

We can breathe in a calming way, connect with supportive friends and disclose our discomfort, express feelings creatively, and so forth. We can show the emotional mind that the rejections and abandonments that felt so intolerable in childhood—and thus vital to avoid in the past—can now be tolerated.

There's no way around feelings: we can only go through them.

Keep sustaining strength.

Be careful when working with desire. It is easy to confuse seduction with a sense of completeness. Not every arising desire must be satisfied. Practice having desire live in the present more than in the future. Otherwise it is yet again a trap of clinging to projected outcomes. Desire must be treated with care and respect and met with kindness and clarity. From this position, test a radically new look one day: How does it feel? With a new look you may encounter a dormant part of yourself, what may even feel like a radically new self. But far too often, we quickly return to the safety of habit. After all, what would my partner/friends/neighbors think?

The question often is how to sustain a new sense of self and cultivate individual strength of character and not fall back into addiction and escape. Like any skill, a self must be practiced. Put the looks of the "new" self easily accessible in the wardrobe, or prepare the night before. Minimize the threshold to make you dress this sense of self. Or set a challenge. On Friday I will be reborn. And then every Friday I dress up for my new birthday.

CHAPTER 5

Fashion in the Bardo

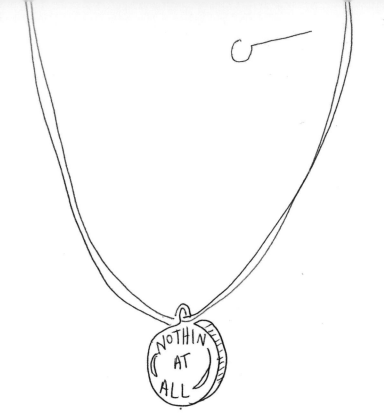

Fashion in the Bardo

Contemplate the life and death of garments.

We move through life with a fragile sense of self. We use clothes to build an identity to appear more solid and permanent: *I am this*. Too many of us are so concerned with building an identity that we have no idea *who* we are under *what* we are. Garments sustain the illusion for only so long, then we need to repeat and reinforce the building process again. So when you lose interest in a garment next time, pay some attention to it before you throw it in the recycling bin.

Think about it: What is it that has "died" in a garment when we throw it out? It may be material qualities, such as holes, stains, or frays, but perhaps more often it is something more abstract: an emotional connection that is gone. Can you spell it out, articulate it to yourself? The question can also be turned around. When is a garment most alive? What is the difference in feeling tones between life and death? How does a garment lose its "breath" or when is its "energy" gone? Write down your reflection.

In the famous *Tibetan Book of the Dead*, a key text for Tibetan Buddhism in the West, the bardo is presented as an intermediate, transitional, or liminal state between death and rebirth. It is a purgatory, a state of limbo. It is a burning intermediate world between two lives on earth where the soul is prepared for rebirth into a new body.

The image of bardo in the *Tibetan Book of the Dead* is popularly known to be full of tormenting demons. They are the horrors the deceased self faces as it is stripped from attachment to old illusions. The demons kill our clinging to the old life, purge us of our comforts and habits, and dismantle our attachments to ego, relations, and possessions. The demons are our helpers; one cannot be reborn if not everything from the old life is taken away so that only pure mind remains.

But the bardo is also a lesson or, more accurately, an opportunity in life. Each transitional reality is a bardo, and they occur continually throughout life, as situations or junctions in life where awareness is heightened and a pathway to liberation is opened. It is a moment when a transition happens and the circumstances are right to unpack its deeper causes and factors. Such bardo can help us reach insight through its teaching moment. Bardo is a chilling reminder of life and death, pushing us to prepare for both, making sure we use the opportunities of life in the best way possible. So for fashion, could it help us prepare for death, and may it prepare us for life?

Reach toward the depth of expression.

In Zen, a teacher's question to a student may be "What was your face before you were born?" Is there an inner nature, behind the mask of selfhood? What is it in you that cannot die, since it was never born? What is this presence that makes a person more than the sum of attributes? This relates to fashion, since it asks you what it is you seek in fashion. Think again; when it is at its best, *how does fashion feel*?

Pay attention to the feeling of fashion you seek. Try to distill it to its essence and write it down. Try to make sure this feeling can be your guiding light in your engagement with fashion; at what times is it the strongest—can you make this experience more lasting? Can it be shared with your friends, experienced on the cheap, and perhaps without environmental cost? Only by truly *feeling fashion* can you touch what fashion is to you.

So, dear reader, let's have a last look at fashion—

a last look into the bardo of selfhood.

Fashion is dead. And dear, I think you feel it too. It is not our fault. It had to be this way. And while it may be of little comfort to all the effort and money you put into your wardrobe, please be assured:

death is not the end.

You are not alone feeling the emptiness and grief. As with all departures, the sense of hollowness comes after the initial denial. Don't ask what caused the death or search for a possible crime scene. We can let others do that. Let's just simply acknowledge the fatal demise.

But dear, the bardo of each garment may also be an opportunity for reckoning. While we stand here dressed, at the end of the line, we may take the moment to look ourselves in the mirror and seek beyond the realm of appearances. Yes, let's take a deeper look at our frailty. It is the cruel finitude that challenges us to reflect on life, and when it comes to fashion we can question why we were so seduced by it, but also what its meaning and purpose can be beyond habits and the cheap thrills.

What is it that fashion frames for our sense of self: a thrill of the new? A sense of exclusivity? A sense of glamour and a moment to almost touch celebrity? A careless one-night stand with consumerism? A magic thrill of shape-shifting? A play between virtue and sin? Dear, what was it we were so seduced by, over and over again?

In the bardo of fashion, each dying garment can offer reflection over our own relationships to desire, craving, and addiction. Yes, let's look into the wardrobe; look at these garments we have lost interest in, where the context no longer seems right, or that we feel our peers no longer approve of. If we dare to reflect on it, each death may expose to us the temporary sense of selfhood that fashion offers, what desires we cling to, and what emotions we are fearful of.

With fashion, as with our fragile love, we drew up contracts and conditions, cultivating an art of performing before each other, feasting in our self-feeding vanity. There was really no room for you in my experience of self; I was so full of myself, so vulnerable to failure. Yet, in the silence I could feel it, the grief, the rage, and anxiety. Such relationship to fashion is an injustice that chokes on the air it breathes; it burns the soul with a passion that leaves no room for healing.

No, it's not the end, dear. Fashion needs to die and be reborn.

Something new must happen between death and rebirth, not just a new look, a new collection, a cute Band-Aid on my decaying corpse. We need this cruel moment to rethink our relation to fashion. Let's try not to be afraid. We may use this opportunity to meditate over fashion's death; over our death.

If this exercise feels abstract, dear, let's make it more concrete. Take out one of the dead garments in your wardrobe, one of those abandoned and unworn pieces at the back shelves. Yes, that shiny top will do fine. Throw it on the floor, ready for the pyre, and let us sit down next to it. Open yourself to the cruel destiny of these remains that were once so full of glimmering dreams and vital desires. This is how the end looks, and a similar fate awaits all of us. Let the destiny of this hollow and broken form seep into you.

This is a corpse to be meditated over.

We will both one day reach this end, too, and be discarded like a rag, thrown into the burning dumpster of time and the oblivion of ephemeral social relationships. As you merge with this fate, accept it, and soon enough you are also dead; you have become one with this old sequined party top. The glimmer is gone, your skin pale, your frailty exposed.

If we imagine that fashion, like the self, holds up an image of its ideal world, it serves a fundamental purpose to most of us, giving us agency to shape our sense of self. Yet, this ideal is corrupted by our attachment to this image. Fashion is attached to our sense of imagined selfhood, and the self is attached back to fashion as an image of the self. We love fashion because we love the image of who we can be, what self we can have; to wish to be seen as just right.

We want fashion to stay as it is, in continuous ascent, just like we want the self to stay as itself, as a process of aesthetic achievements. Like in the bardo, we keep postponing our acceptance of the rupture, just to sustain the illusion that reality is just as we imagine it should be. We need more demons to torment us, to strip away all images of self. Dear, let us burn our egos. They must be scorched for something new to grow. Oh, even my modest vanity needs to go. And the hip supremacy of my Supreme shirts. Bring me some more fire.

In the bardo of fashion we strip fashion down from its skins of ego and illusion. Peel off the layers of attachment to our success. Purge the glamour and pride that comes with the expensive goods. Strip off all those layers of coolness, irony, and arrogance. Burn these limited-edition sneakers too. Let the demons flay our corpses of idolatry and narcissism. Embrace the fire and let the smoldering sulfur replace your expensive fragrance. Clean away your conception of fashion from its consumerist self—let it no longer be tainted by social anxiety and the imperative to perform and achieve. Let the demons strip off the ego; it is painful.

Hold on, dear; wait for me – I am not there yet.

Finally, the fire soothes; the tormented screams die out. It is all gone. Fashion is thoroughly dead. Let us embrace; we reached the middle point. We can rest awhile at this plateau. Now, let's search through the aches of the self, among the burnt shells of our enclothed pride, attachment, craving, and envy. Let's look together; what can we find?

Is there any trace left of what we once called fashion?

After the demons of bardo have stripped away illusions of self, there is still something left; it is presence. Nothing more than pure presence: the smallest cinder of being. This is the presence that forms the very basics of mind and interconnected being. Can we also find a small ember left in the ashes of fashion? Is there something left worthy of rebirth? Perhaps what remains of fashion is our shared attention, a presence manifesting itself between two people. A presence of being, of being with another; a sense of togetherness. Is this the ember of fashion, a fashion stripped of narcissist illusions of selfhood? Is this the ember we want to save for a new life?

Following the cleansing in bardo, a new self is born from presence. This is the new beginning, a new point of departure. From this presence we start building a new life, a new relationship to fashion. It can be a new fashion that starts from the attention toward another being. Can our new mutual attention be another form of sensuous flirting, beyond the corrupting forces of craving, clinging, and aversion?

Fashion in the Bardo

Can it be a presence transcending our need to control the recipient of love? It has to be the spaciousness that opens as I withdraw my ego to open up a room between us, to let you into my life without expectations. It has to be a fashion that is about healing and the courage to love, to let down the guard and take pleasure in our shared desires.

My love, fashion is dead. But death is not the end, dear. Fashion is the process of continuous rebirth, because it is a fire that burns all life.

Dear, you are amazing. And you look wonderful in that old party top. We can have a moment together and say goodbye. Let's embrace one last time, before the light in those glimmering sequins goes out.

Otto

tto von Busch is an associate professor of integrated design at Parsons School of Design. He holds a PhD in design from the School of Design and Craft at the University of Gothenburg, Sweden, and has taught and exhibited work on topics of fashion and empowerment over the last fifteen years. He has a background in arts, craft, design, and theory, and his projects explore how design, and especially fashion, can mobilize community capabilities through collaborative craft and social activism. Find more of his work at www.selfpassage.info

von

Busch